D0724502

_____

_____

From:

_____

_____

Message:

_____

_____

_____

_____

101 Prayers for my Daughter

CHRISTIAN ART
PUBLISHERS

Published by Christian Art Publishers
PO Box 1599, Vereeniging, 1930, RSA

© 2016
First edition 2016

Cover designed by Christian Art Publishers

Images used under license from Shutterstock.com

Scripture quotations are taken from the *Holy Bible*,
New International Version® NIV®. Copyright © 1973,
1978, 1984, 2011 by International Bible Society.
Used by permission of Biblica, Inc.®
All rights reserved worldwide.

Printed in China

ISBN 978-1-4321-1348-3

17 18 19 20 21 22 23 24 25 26 – 13 12 11 10 9 8 7 6 5 4

Children

are a **heritage**

from the LORD,

offspring a reward

from Him.

Psalm 127:3

01

Assurance of Salvation

Jesus said to her,
"I am the resurrection and the life.
The one who believes in Me will live,
even though they die; and whoever lives
by believing in Me will never die.
Do you believe this?"

John 11:25-26

Lord God,

I pray that my daughter would believe in
Jesus with all of her heart. Open her eyes
to see that life is found through faith in
You alone. Let my precious child become
Your child as well. Give us the hope of
eternity spent together with You – and
each other – as we put our trust in You.

Amen.

02

Friends for Life

Two are better than one,
because they have a good return
for their labor: If either of them falls
down, one can help the other up.
But pity anyone who falls and
has no one to help them up.

Ecclesiastes 4:9-10

Lord,

My daughter needs a friend. It's painful
to feel left out and alone. When hard days
come, there's no one to care and offer an
encouraging word. Give her someone to
stay by her side and help her up when she
falls down. Let her experience Your faithful
love through the joy of a true friend
that loves her too.

Amen.

Peaceful Rest | 03

In peace I will lie down
and sleep, for You alone, LORD,
make me dwell in safety.

Psalm 4:8

Father God,

My daughter is struggling to sleep.
Stress and worry make peaceful rest
impossible. Pour out the gift of sweet sleep
that will refresh her body and spirit. Quiet
her anxious thoughts and agitation. Keep
Your faithful watch over my child, so she
can find perfect peace and rest
in Your loving care.

Amen.

04 | A Humble Heart

Do nothing out of selfish ambition
or vain conceit. Rather, in humility value
others above yourselves, not looking
to your own interests but each of you
to the interests of the others.

Philippians 2:3-4

Lord God,

You've blessed my daughter with
intelligence, talent and creativity.
Keep her from using these gifts to
seek praise and attention for herself.
Give her a humble heart that can celebrate
the achievements of others. Help her to
recognize that her strengths come from
You, in order to make her a blessing.
Be glorified as she lifts others up
and serves in Your name.

Amen.

05

Patience in Everything

My dear brothers and sisters, take note of
this: Everyone should be quick to listen,
slow to speak and slow to become angry,
because human anger does not produce
the righteousness that God desires.

James 1:19-20

Father,

My daughter lashes out when she's angry,
without considering how she might hurt
other people. Teach her to listen and think
before she responds to the frustrations that
come her way. Give her patience to bear
with others' weaknesses. Humble her heart
to gracefully receive correction. Set her free
from the trap of a quick temper, so she
can grow in Your righteousness.

Amen.

06

Her Prayer Life

In the morning, LORD, You hear my voice;
in the morning I lay my requests
before You and wait expectantly.

Psalm 5:3

Lord,

Teach my daughter to pray. Let her seek You
every morning of her life. Help her to place
every problem in Your hands. Give her faith
to believe You will hear and answer. Set her
free from fear and doubt that will keep her
far from You. Respond to her prayers with
Your loving power – You will do more
than she can ask or imagine.

Amen.

Healing Touch | 07

Heal me, LORD, and I will be healed;
save me and I will be saved,
for You are the one I praise.

Jeremiah 17:14

Father,

When my daughter is sick and weary,
restore her strength and encourage
her spirit. Save her from doubting Your
goodness and power. Teach her to rest in
You, believing You are in control. Give
her endurance to bear the pain. May
Your perfect work of healing bring
praise to Your name.

Amen.

08 | The Truth of God

Love does not delight in evil
but rejoices with the truth.

1 Corinthians 13:6

Lord God,

I pray that my daughter would live in
Your truth. Renew her mind by Your perfect
Word. Fill her mouth with honest words
that glorify You. Keep her heart free from
deception and secrecy. Give her integrity to
keep her promises and admit her mistakes.
Protect her from the confusion of false
teaching. Let her love You more and more
as she finds You always faithful and true.

Amen.

09

Modesty & Goodness

I also want the women to dress modestly,
with decency and propriety, adorning
themselves, not with elaborate hairstyles
or gold or pearls or expensive clothes,
but with good deeds, appropriate for
women who profess to worship God.

1 Timothy 2:9-10

Father God,

Let my daughter's beauty come from
a spirit of humility, generosity and love.
Guard her heart from craving attention
through fashion and sex appeal. Give her
courage to submit to Your will and Your
ways, even if she doesn't fit in with the
crowd. May her modesty and goodness
be an act of worship as she devotes
herself to You in everything she does.

Amen.

10

Obedience & Instruction

Children, obey your parents in
the Lord, for this is right. "Honor
your father and mother" – which is the
first commandment with a promise –
"so that it may go well with you and that
you may enjoy long life on the earth."

Ephesians 6:1-3

O Lord,

Open the door to blessing for my daughter
as she learns to obey. Give her a humble
heart that can submit to my instructions.
Make her teachable, avoiding pain and
trouble by following my direction. Give
her an honoring attitude, and make me
worthy of her respect. May she obey me
out of love for You, for Your name's sake.

Amen.

Contentment & Gratitude | 11

You desire but do not have, so you kill.
You covet but you cannot get what you want,
so you quarrel and fight. You do not have
because you do not ask God.

James 4:2

Lord,

Guard my daughter's heart from jealousy.
Fill her with gratitude instead of craving
the blessings of others. Let her bring every
desire to You in prayer instead of fighting
for what she wants. Give her patience to
wait for every good thing You have in store
for her. Thank You for lavishing Your love on
my daughter – may she praise Your name!

Amen.

12 | A Life of Peace

"Blessed are the peacemakers,
for they will be called children of God."

Matthew 5:9

Father,

Let my daughter pursue peace with
everyone. Give her humility to admit
when she's wrong and the strength to
make amends. Help her to forgive when
she's offended, seeking reconciliation
instead of revenge. Restore her
relationships as she learns patience,
compassion and love by Your Spirit.

Amen.

13

A Godly Life

His divine power has given us everything
we need for a godly life through our
knowledge of Him who called us
by His own glory and goodness.

2 Peter 1:3

Lord God,

I pray that my daughter would live in
obedience to You. Fill her mind with an
ever-growing knowledge of You and Your
Word. Strengthen her by Your power to
accomplish every purpose and plan You've
created for her life. Let her righteousness
and goodness shine as a light in this dark
world. May she bring glory to Your
name as she lives for You.

Amen.

14

Happiness & Joy

May the righteous be glad and rejoice
before God; may they be happy and joyful.

Psalm 68:3

Father,

Fill my daughter with happiness and joy.
Open her eyes to see Your gifts and her
heart to rejoice in Your love. Give her
a cheerful spirit that is grateful in every
situation, trusting that You are with her.
Use her positive attitude to encourage
others when they're feeling down. Be her
greatest delight – knowing You is better
than any pleasure this world can hold.

Amen.

Her Self-Worth | 15

You created my inmost being; You
knit me together in my mother's womb.
I praise You because I am fearfully and
wonderfully made; Your works are
wonderful, I know that full well.

Psalm 139:13-14

Lord Jesus,

Thank You for creating my beautiful
daughter. You planned every detail
of her personality, her intellect and her
appearance. Give her faith to believe she is
a wonderful, incredible work of God Himself.
May she be convinced of her important
place in this world – that she is destined by
You, cherished by me, and loved through
and through by her heavenly Father.

Amen.

16 | Comfort from Above

**The LORD is close to the brokenhearted
and saves those who are crushed in spirit.**

Psalm 34:18

Father,

Draw near to my daughter in times
of difficulty. Let her rest in You and bring
all her troubles to You. Where sadness and
doubt consume her thoughts, bring peace
and faith that You're in control. Where she is
tired and discouraged, renew her strength
and hope for tomorrow. Thank You for
holding my daughter in Your arms.

Amen.

17

Diligence in All She Does

Whatever you do, work at it with all your heart, as working for the Lord, not for human masters, since you know that you will receive an inheritance from the Lord as a reward. It is the Lord Christ you are serving.

Colossians 3:23-24

Lord God,

Give my daughter the strength to accomplish all that is before her today. Fill her with courage when the work seems too difficult. Help her persevere to the end, leaning on You when she's tired or discouraged. Capture her heart with a desire to serve You above anyone else. Let her receive Your wonderful rewards for her diligence and obedience today.

Amen.

18

An Unshakable Faith

Without faith it is impossible to please God, because anyone who comes to Him must believe that He exists and that He rewards those who earnestly seek Him.

Hebrews 11:6

Lord,

Fill my daughter's heart with an insatiable longing for You. May she seek You earnestly and discover the rewards You have in store. When the world denies Your Word and rejects Jesus, give her strength to hold on to the truth. Replace her doubts with assurance, and her confusion with clarity. Be pleased with my daughter as she grows in faith and trust.

Amen.

Her Treasure | 19

"Store up for yourselves treasures in heaven, where moths and vermin do not destroy, and where thieves do not break in and steal. For where your treasure is, there your heart will be also."

Matthew 6:20-21

Father,

Guard my daughter's heart from the love of money. May she place her hope in You, trusting in Your faithfulness to meet every need. Let her live to build Your kingdom instead of her bank account. Give her a spirit of gratitude and generosity so she can share Your blessings with others. Keep her eyes fixed on You – expectantly waiting for eternity with You in heaven.

Amen.

20 | Freedom from Pride

Live in harmony with one another.
Do not be proud, but be willing
to associate with people of low
position. Do not be conceited.

Romans 12:16

Father,

Teach my daughter to be a true friend.
Keep her from pride and selfishness that
strives for popularity. Give her a loving heart
that reaches out to others, regardless of
how they fit in with the crowd. Use her as
a peacemaker so that no one is left out or
rejected. May her kindness and compassion
shine the light of Jesus wherever she goes.

Amen.

21

Worship & Praise

I rejoiced with those who said to me,
"Let us go to the house of the Lord."

Psalm 122:1

Lord God,

I pray that my daughter would love
Your church. Give her joy as she gathers
with other believers to worship. Let her
experience Your presence as the Word is
preached and praises are lifted up in prayer
and singing. Envelop her in love through
the ministry of Your people. Use the church
to build her faith and knowledge of You.

Amen.

22

Bless Her Future Marriage

"'For this reason a man will leave his father and mother and be united to his wife, and the two will become one flesh.' So they are no longer two, but one flesh. Therefore what God has joined together, let no one separate."

Mark 10:7-9

Father,

Even now, prepare my daughter and her future husband for their life together. Build them up in faith so they can live in obedience to You. Give them an unshakable commitment to each other that will stand the test of time. When disappointments, troubles and temptations come their way, let them lean on You and hold fast to one another. Give them unity by Your Spirit that can never be broken.

Amen.

Spiritual Protection | 23

Be alert and of sober mind.
Your enemy the devil prowls around
like a roaring lion looking for someone
to devour. Resist him, standing firm in
the faith, because you know that the family
of believers throughout the world is
undergoing the same kind of sufferings.

1 Peter 5:8-9

Lord God,

Guard my daughter from the enemy –
he wants to make her suffer and destroy her
life. Give her discernment to detect his lies
and schemes. Fill her with courage to resist
him, believing Your Word and trusting in
Your love. May she flee temptation, live in
Your truth, and stand firm in the faith
without wavering. Surround her with
believers so she doesn't have to
face the enemy alone.

Amen.

24 | Repentance & Forgiveness

Whoever conceals their sins does not
prosper, but the one who confesses
and renounces them finds mercy.

Proverbs 28:13

Holy Father,

Humble my daughter's heart to admit
whenever she makes a mistake. Fill her with
godly sorrow that will keep her from rest
until she's confessed her sin to You. Help
her to trust in Your mercy and promises
to forgive. Let her commit her way to You,
turning from the path of sin and back to
obedience. Bring her healing and joy
as she gives herself fully to You.

Amen.

25

Her Worries

"Why do you worry about clothes?
See how the flowers of the field grow.
They do not labor or spin. Yet I tell you that
not even Solomon in all his splendor was
dressed like one of these."

Matthew 6:28-29

Lord Jesus,

Guard my daughter's heart from worry
about clothes. She longs for acceptance
and could place hope in her appearance
instead of You. Set her free from the
pressure to keep up and fit in with the
world's definition of beauty. Give her
contentment and a thankful heart for
what You've provided in her closet.
Let her trust You to meet her needs
since You care for every detail of her life.

Amen.

26

Friends in Faith

I do not sit with the deceitful,
nor do I associate with hypocrites.
I abhor the assembly of evildoers
and refuse to sit with the wicked.

Psalm 26:4-5

Father,

Give my daughter wisdom in choosing her
friends. Open her eyes to discern those who
live out their faith from their heart instead of
just empty religion. Keep her from joining
in with gossip or competing for popularity.
Give her a gentle, kind spirit to keep her
from taking part in bullying, or excluding
or slandering another person. Use her as
a peacemaker to stand up for what's right,
showing the love of Jesus to everyone.

Amen.

Submission to Authority | 27

Let everyone be subject to the governing
authorities, for there is no authority except
that which God has established.
The authorities that exist have been
established by God.

Romans 13:1

Lord God,

Give my daughter strength to submit to the
leaders of her church, school, community
and nation. May she understand that
limits and laws are in place for her safety
and well-being. Help her to show self-
control when tempted to drive recklessly,
disrespect property or insult authority. May
she follow the rules out of obedience to
You, trusting You are in control. Reward
her with honor and peace.

Amen.

28 | A Willing Heart

Do everything without grumbling or arguing, so that you may become blameless and pure, "children of God without fault in a warped and crooked generation."

Philippians 2:14-15

Heavenly Father,

I pray that my daughter would have a willing heart to follow wherever You lead. Give her strength to tackle challenging tasks and assignments without complaining. Let her help and serve others with a cheerful spirit. When she faces hard times, give her courage and endurance to make it through. May she obey You in all things with a pure heart, shining Your light in these dark days.

Amen.

29

Wisdom with Her Words

A gossip betrays a confidence,
but a trustworthy person keeps a secret.
Proverbs 11:13

Lord,

Give my daughter wisdom with her words.
Let her friends have confidence in her
integrity and respect. Help her to resist
temptation to share secrets and gossip.
Give her discernment to recognize who she
can trust with her personal life. Guard her
from slander and gossip that can damage
her reputation and ruin relationships.
Bless her with an upright heart as You
keep her secure in Your love.

Amen.

30

Intimacy with God

"Do not fear, for I have redeemed you; I have summoned you by name; you are Mine."

Isaiah 43:1

Father God,

I confess that I am terrified my daughter will never know You. Replace my fear with trust, to believe that You will call her to Yourself. Claim her as Your own – may her name be written in heaven in the Book of Life. Give her ears to hear Your words of love, and eyes to see Your presence. Break down every barrier that is keeping her from running to You. Replace her doubts with faith that will last.

Amen.

Freedom from Addiction | 31

"I have the right to do anything," you say –
but not everything is beneficial. "I have
the right to do anything" – but I will
not be mastered by anything.

1 Corinthians 6:12

Lord,

It's tempting for my daughter to seek
comfort in the pleasures of this world,
rather than You. Keep her from dependence
on food, sex, shopping, entertainment,
drugs, relationships, alcohol – anything
that falsely promises peace or happiness.
Protect my daughter and set her free
from any addiction that could ruin her life.
Be her strength and her source of
joy in every moment.

Amen.

32 | Direction for Her Life

Your word is a lamp for my feet,
a light on my path.

Psalm 119:105

Father,

My daughter is at a crossroads;
she doesn't know which way to go.
Move her heart to desire Your perfect plan.
Speak through Your Word so she knows
which path to take. Help her to understand
how Scripture applies to her life as she
makes choices from day to day. Let her
walk in Your light without stumbling in
the darkness of this world. Give her
faithful guidance for every step.

Amen.

33

Her Image

Charm is deceptive, and beauty is fleeting;
but a woman who fears the LORD
is to be praised.

Proverbs 31:30

Righteous Father,

The world tells my daughter that her worth
is found in her appearance. Guard her
heart and mind from believing that beauty
depends on perfect skin, hair and the size
of her jeans. Give her peace when she's
worried about looking just right. Let her
please You instead of trying to live up to
people's expectations. Fill her with Your
beauty – perfect love that never ends.

Amen.

34

How to Discipline Her

Discipline your children,
and they will give you peace;
they will bring you the delights you desire.

Proverbs 29:17

Lord,

Show me how to discipline my
daughter with wisdom and love. Use
the consequences of her actions to train
her in obedience. Keep me from anger that
seeks to punish rather than to help and
guide. Make me courageous in holding
to what's right, even if she argues and
complains. Reward us with peace and
joy as my daughter does what's right.

Amen.

A Generous Heart | 35

Each of you should give what
you have decided in your heart to give,
not reluctantly or under compulsion,
for God loves a cheerful giver.

2 Corinthians 9:7

Lord God,

You lavish Your love upon us – give Your
heart of generosity to my daughter. Make
her eager to share her blessings instead of
hoarding Your gifts for herself. Let her share
out of a pure heart, finding joy in giving to
anyone in need. Guard her from selfishness
that will keep her from loving others and
shining Your light. Fill her with thanks for
the good things that come from Your hand.

Amen.

36 | A Good Reputation

A good name is more desirable
than great riches; to be esteemed is
better than silver or gold.

Proverbs 22:1

Father,

Keep my daughter's reputation
safely in Your hands. Protect her from
slander and lies that would tear her down.
Give her wisdom and self-control so that
impulsive choices don't ruin her good
name. Surround her with friends who walk
in goodness and truth. Make her a young
woman of honor, showing integrity in
every situation. Let her be known for her
character as she commits her way to You.

Amen.

37

Strength When Suffering Persecution

"Blessed are you when people insult you,
persecute you and falsely say all kinds
of evil against you because of Me."

Matthew 5:11

Holy Lord,

Living for You will make my daughter stand
out in this world. Give her strength to hold
firmly to her faith even if she walks alone.
Encourage her heart when she's rejected,
insulted or harassed for following Jesus.
Give her compassion for Your people who
suffer abuse and even death as Christians.
Protect her from fear and pour out blessings
in her life when she suffers in Your name.

Amen.

38

Her Training

Start children off on the way they should go,
and even when they are old they
will not turn from it.

Proverbs 22:6

Father,

Give me wisdom in how to teach and train
my daughter. Show me how to encourage
her talents and develop the strengths of
her personality. Let me guide her in the
truth of Your Word as she grows. Allow
our relationship to flourish so my love and
influence remain a blessing in her life.
Bring her to maturity, firmly established
on the path You've laid out for her future.
Thank You for the privilege of raising
my precious daughter.

Amen.

Being Bullied | 39

"But I tell you, love your enemies and pray
for those who persecute you, that you may
be children of your Father in heaven."

Matthew 5:44-45

Lord,

You loved us first, when we were lost in our
sins and didn't love You at all. I pray that my
daughter would have Your heart, and love
her enemies. Fill her with kindness and
compassion when she's bullied or insulted.
Teach her to pray for those who come
against her – that they would turn to Jesus
and find peace. Give her patience and
courage to remain loving through it all.

Amen.

40 | True Beauty

Your beauty should not come from outward adornment, such as elaborate hairstyles and the wearing of gold jewelry or fine clothes. Rather, it should be that of your inner self, the unfading beauty of a gentle and quiet spirit, which is of great worth in God's sight.

1 Peter 3:3-4

Righteous Father,

Guard my daughter from defining her beauty by what she sees in the mirror. Let her look past the outer display of fashion, hair and makeup, and value what's in the heart. Help her to be gentle and quiet instead of showing off to get attention. Keep her from judging other girls by their appearance. Give her a peaceful, tender spirit that is lovely for all to see.

Amen.

41

A Firm Faith in Jesus

See to it that no one takes you captive
through hollow and deceptive philosophy,
which depends on human tradition
and the elemental spiritual forces of
this world rather than on Christ.

Colossians 2:8

Lord Jesus,

The enemy and the world want to
replace Your truth with lies. My daughter
might hear that salvation is found in rituals
or traditions instead of Jesus. She might be
pressured to deny You as her authority
and the Creator of the world. Protect her
from believing anyone who would turn
her away from You and Your Word.
Guard her heart from doubt. Keep her
secure in a faith that can't be shaken.

Amen.

42

A Forgiving Heart

Do not repay evil with evil or insult
with insult. On the contrary, repay evil with
blessing, because to this you were called so
that you may inherit a blessing.

1 Peter 3:9

Lord,

Any insult makes my daughter want
to lash out with rudeness of her own.
A push leads to a shove. Gossip stirs up
more gossip. Move in my daughter's heart
so she can love others instead of taking
revenge. Let her show patience and
forgiveness instead of fighting for her
rights. May she receive Your blessings
as she becomes a blessing to others.

Amen.

Compassion like Jesus | 43

Therefore, as God's chosen people,
holy and dearly loved, clothe yourselves
with compassion, kindness, humility,
gentleness and patience.

Colossians 3:12

Father,

Give my daughter Your heart of
compassion for everyone. Soften her
heart for the hurting. Use her to care for the
sick, the poor and the outcast. Let her treat
others as special and important. Help her to
be gentle, even when she's treated harshly.
Give her patience when she's provoked or
treated unfairly. Bring Your kindness and
love to the world through her life.

Amen.

44 | Doing Good

Let us not become weary in doing good, for at the proper time we will reap a harvest if we do not give up. Therefore, as we have opportunity, let us do good to all people, especially to those who belong to the family of believers.

Galatians 6:9-10

Lord,

Show my daughter how she can be a blessing in this world. Teach her to give to the poor, encourage the hurting and help the weak. Open her eyes to see the ways she can share Your love. Give her strength to keep on giving and serving, even when she's tired or feels unappreciated. Let her discover Your beautiful rewards for doing good.

Amen.

45

An Inquisitive Mind

Apply your heart to instruction
and your ears to words of knowledge.
Proverbs 23:12

Holy Lord,

Give my daughter an eager, inquisitive
mind that loves to learn. Help her to value
her education and commit to her studies.
When the work is challenging, give her
strength to finish well. Surround her with
wise teachers who will encourage her
along the way. Equip her to serve You with
the skills and knowledge she receives.
Guide her steps, fill her mind with truth,
and reward her with wisdom and success.

Amen.

46

Respecting Authority

Children, obey your parents in everything,
for this pleases the Lord.

Colossians 3:20

Father,

My daughter sometimes struggles to
obey what I ask her to do. She can be
disrespectful and resistant to my authority,
keeping peace from our home. Help her
to submit herself to Your design for family
by honoring me as her parent. Give her a
cheerful, humble attitude so she can listen
and cooperate. Give me wisdom, love
and patience as she learns obedience.
Let my daughter be pleasing to You.

Amen.

Care for Animals | 47

The righteous care for the needs of their
animals, but the kindest acts of
the wicked are cruel.

Proverbs 12:10

Father of all,

Thank You for Your beautiful creation
and the living creatures we enjoy. Give my
daughter a compassionate heart that seeks
to protect the animals You've made. Teach
her to be diligent in caring for her pets.
Let her stand up for weak and abandoned
animals that have no defense. As she loves
Your created world, let her tender heart be
a witness of Your great love for everyone.

Amen.

48 | Standing Up for Others

My whole being will exclaim, "Who is like You, LORD? You rescue the poor from those too strong for them, the poor and needy from those who rob them."

Psalm 35:10

Lord God,

Your power and love are wonderful! You stand up for the weak and rescue us from trouble. Give Your heart of mercy to my daughter. Give her strength to stand up for those who can't defend themselves. Fill her hands with blessings so she can share with the poor and needy. Make her courageous to fight every kind of injustice and oppression – living out Your love and truth in this world.

Amen.

49

Easing Her Anxiety

Anxiety weighs down the heart,
but a kind word cheers it up.

Proverbs 12:25

Lord,

My daughter can become paralyzed by
stress and fear. She worries about her
friendships, her grades, her safety and her
future. Doubts and insecurities steal her
happiness. Let Your love and peace melt
away her anxieties. Help her to trust You
in every situation. Give her joy as she finds
You faithful. Give me encouraging words to
build her up and put a smile on her face.

Amen.

50

Liberty from Depression

Why, my soul, are you downcast?
Why so disturbed within me? Put your
hope in God, for I will yet praise
Him, my Savior and my God.

Psalm 42:5

Father,

My daughter doesn't always cope so
well with her struggles. In times like these,
depression steals her joy. Fill her with hope
by Your Spirit. Give her faith to believe You
will never leave her side. Let her trust in
Your love, knowing You are everything
she needs. Open her eyes to see Your
goodness, and let her praise Your
name as You lift her up.

Amen.

Living in Unity | 51

How good and pleasant it is when God's
people live together in unity!

Psalm 133:1

Lord God,

Conflict, competition and criticism are
spoiling the peace in our home. Fill my
daughter with love so she'll work to get
along with others. Help her to desire good
things for everyone instead of having her
own way. Let her show respect for people's
ideas and opinions. Give her a forgiving spirit
when she's offended. Enable my daughter to
be a peacemaker, encourager and helper to
her family and friends each day.

Amen.

52 | Her Witness

In your hearts revere Christ as Lord.
Always be prepared to give an answer to
everyone who asks you to give the reason
for the hope that you have.

1 Peter 3:15

Holy Father,

I pray that my daughter would love You with
all of her heart, her soul and her strength.
Fill her with hope, flowing out of the joy of
knowing Jesus. Give her the words to say
when she's asked to explain her trust in You.
Keep her from any fear or embarrassment
about sharing what You've done in her life.
Use my daughter to shine the light of the
gospel in this lost and hurting world.

Amen.

53

God's Goodness

Children are a heritage from the LORD,
offspring a reward from Him.

Psalm 127:3

Lord Jesus,

Thank You for the gift of my daughter.
You created her in Your image, and she's
beautifully and wonderfully made. Help me
to remember she was especially chosen
for me and our family. Give me a heart that
cherishes her as a reward from You. Knit us
together in love, building a strong relationship that will last. May I always praise Your
name for Your goodness to me – my
daughter is a precious blessing from You.

Amen.

54

God's Creation

Since the creation of the world God's
invisible qualities – His eternal power
and divine nature – have been clearly seen,
being understood from what has been made,
so that people are without excuse.

Romans 1:20

Lord,

Open my daughter's eyes to see how
You're revealed in Your creation. Let the
beauty and majesty of nature touch her
heart and move her to worship You. Use
her studies and knowledge of the natural
world to confirm that You are the Creator
of all things. Build her faith in You, our
invisible God, through this marvelous
universe You've made.

Amen.

Changing a Critical Nature | 55

"How can you say to your brother, 'Brother, let me take the speck out of your eye,' when you yourself fail to see the plank in your own eye? You hypocrite, first take the plank out of your eye, and then you will see clearly to remove the speck from your brother's eye."

Luke 6:42

Holy Lord,

My daughter can sometimes be quick to point out the mistakes and weaknesses of others. Give her a humble heart to see how she needs to grow and change before she criticizes people around her. Give her patience and mercy by Your Spirit. Let her long for goodness and obedience, to become more like Jesus every day. Inspire others to follow You by the love she displays in her life.

Amen.

56 | A Heart of Compassion

"To you who are listening I say:
Love your enemies, do good to those
who hate you, bless those who curse you,
pray for those who mistreat you."

Luke 6:27-28

Heavenly Father,

My daughter feels angry and hurt when she's
rejected, teased or insulted. She builds a wall
around her heart and pulls away from others.
She tends to hold on to grudges and refuses
to give second chances. Help her to show
compassion and to forgive. Let her show
kindness by blessing and praying for her
enemies. Through Jesus' love and strength,
may she give grace and pursue peace
with everyone in her life.

Amen.

57

Knowing Jesus' Voice

"My sheep listen to My voice;
I know them, and they follow Me. I give
them eternal life, and they shall never perish;
no one will snatch them out of My hand."

John 10:27-28

Father,

Teach my daughter to recognize Your voice.
Let her hear You when she prays and reads
Your Word. Even when the world tries to
drown You out, let her respond to Your call
and follow You every day. Help her to trust
that You will never let her go. As she suffers
through any kind of struggle or temptation,
let her know she's Yours as You hold her
securely in Your hand.

Amen.

58

Peace & Reconciliation

"If you are offering your gift at
the altar and there remember that your
brother or sister has something against you,
leave your gift there in front of the altar.
First go and be reconciled to them;
then come and offer your gift."

Matthew 5:23-24

Lord God,

My daughter isn't perfect – she will make
mistakes and let people down. She'll hurt
others with her words and actions. Give
her a loving heart that craves peace and
reconciliation. Let her admit when she's
wrong and seek forgiveness. Supply her
with strength to make amends and rebuild
broken relationships. Bless her with
peace by Your Spirit.

Amen.

Let us behave decently, as in
the daytime, not in carousing and
drunkenness, not in sexual immorality
and debauchery, not in dissension and
jealousy. Rather, clothe yourselves with the
Lord Jesus Christ, and do not think about
how to gratify the desires of the flesh.

Romans 13:13-14

Father God,

My daughter will at times be tempted
to seek happiness in partying, sexual
experiences and material possessions. Give
her strength to resist the traps of drugs and
alcohol. Guard her innocence. Give her
wisdom in knowing where to look for fun and
adventure. Fill her with gratitude for what
You've given her, so she doesn't depend
on money or "things" to satisfy. Let her
life be conformed to the holiness of Jesus.

Amen.

60 | Confession & Prayer

Confess your sins to each other
and pray for each other so that you may
be healed. The prayer of a righteous person
is powerful and effective.

James 5:16

Lord,

Give my daughter a sensitive conscience
that grieves when she disobeys You. Show
her how freedom and blessings come
through sharing her weaknesses with others.
Provide godly people to pray for her and
build her up. Give me wisdom as her parent,
faithfully praying and helping her overcome
her sins. Move through our prayers to bring
Your healing and power into her life.

Amen.

61

Protection from a Cruel World

Keep me safe from the traps set by evildoers,
from the snares they have laid for me.
Let the wicked fall into their own nets,
while I pass by in safety.

Psalm 141:9-10

Father,

Guard my daughter from any
schemes to do her harm or make
her stumble. Protect her from online
predators who would exploit her innocence.
Keep her safe from bullying, damaging lies
and cruelty. Deliver her from destructive
influences that tempt her to disobey
Your Word. Surround her with Your
angels everywhere she goes, that
no evil person may touch her.

Amen.

62

Training Her in Goodness

A rod and a reprimand impart wisdom,
but a child left undisciplined
disgraces its mother.

Proverbs 29:15

Father,

Teach me how to discipline my
daughter as she grows. Show me how
to train her in goodness and godliness.
Give me wisdom in using rewards and
consequences to shape her choices. When
I'm weary of the work of parenting, build
me up with strength to keep on teaching
my child. Let my discipline bear fruit in her
life, that she may live in obedience to You.

Amen.

Resisting Peer Pressure | 63

Am I now trying to win the approval of
human beings, or of God? Or am I trying to
please people? If I were still trying to please
people, I would not be a servant of Christ.

Galatians 1:10

Lord,

There may be times when my daughter
might be tempted to betray her conscience
to fit in with the crowd. She could feel
pressure to conform to the world's definition
of what's fun, attractive and true. Give my
daughter courage to live as a servant of
Christ. Make it her heart's desire to please
You in everything, instead of trying to live
up to people's expectations. Set her free
to live in joyful obedience to You.

Amen.

64 | Her Gifts

If your gift is prophesying, then prophesy
in accordance with your faith; if it is serving,
then serve; if it is teaching, then teach; if it
is to encourage, then give encouragement;
if it is giving, then give generously; if
it is to lead, do it diligently; if it is
to show mercy, do it cheerfully.

Romans 12:6-8

Father,

Thank You for equipping us with
strengths and abilities through the power
of Your Spirit. Give my daughter wisdom
to recognize how she can serve Your
people and bless the world for Jesus. Fill
her with joy when she helps, shares, teaches
or builds up others who are in need of Your
love. May she depend on You to provide all
she needs to do Your work, for Your glory.

Amen.

65

Her Dreams

Hope deferred makes the heart sick,
but a longing fulfilled is a tree of life.

Proverbs 13:12

Lord God,

My daughter is waiting for her dreams to
come true. It's a struggle to have patience
and believe that good things will come in
Your perfect timing. Encourage her heart by
Your love. Shape the desires and hopes of
her heart so that she will seek Your perfect
will. Give her faith to believe that You
are always good and faithful.

Amen.

66

Restoring
Hope & Strength

Praise the LORD, my soul, and forget not
all His benefits – who forgives all your sins
and heals all your diseases, who redeems
your life from the pit and crowns you
with love and compassion.

Psalm 103:2-4

Father,

In this broken world, my daughter's heart
will be wounded and her body will suffer
sickness and injury. Hold her tenderly and
bring Your comfort in the pain. Restore her
hope and strength. Let her discover Your
perfect love that heals as she cries out to
You. Give her endurance to wait patiently
for You as her great Physician.

Amen.

Faith like a Child | 67

Jesus called the children to Him and said,
"Let the little children come to Me, and do
not hinder them, for the kingdom of
God belongs to such as these."

Luke 18:16

Father God,

Thank You for cherishing my daughter,
allowing her to love You and to know Your
name. Give her a desire to come to You and
worship. Tear down any barrier that would
keep her from You. Never allow any person
to discourage her from seeking Your face.
Build up an unshakable faith in her
young heart so that she will trust
in You forever.

Amen.

68 | Appreciating What She Has

Then Jesus said to them,
"Watch out! Be on your guard against all
kinds of greed; life does not consist in
an abundance of possessions."

Luke 12:15

Righteous Lord,

Nothing will destroy my daughter's joy
and gratitude like a greedy heart. Fill her
with appreciation for all You've done in her
life. Open her eyes to see Your blessings,
and the contentment to be fully satisfied.
Guard her heart from loving Your gifts
above You, the Giver. Let her discover true
happiness in You as her loving Father.

Amen.

69

Wisdom from God

If any of you lacks wisdom, you should ask God, who gives generously to all without finding fault, and it will be given to you.

James 1:5

Lord,

My daughter needs Your direction as she makes choices in life. Help her to know which way to go as she makes plans for her education, career and relationships. Give her a heart that seeks Your will, wanting to please You above herself. Let her trust Your guidance when she's confused or in doubt about the next steps to take.

Amen.

70

Knowing God's Love

And I pray that you, being rooted and established in love, may have power, together with all the Lord's holy people, to grasp how wide and long and high and deep is the love of Christ, and to know this love that surpasses knowledge – that you may be filled to the measure of all the fullness of God.

Ephesians 3:17-19

Holy Father,

When trials come or the evil in this world seems overwhelming, my daughter may doubt that You're really in control. She may wonder if Your light will overcome the darkness. Give her the power to comprehend that Your love is greater than we can imagine. Fill her to overflowing with the fullness of God. Overwhelm her life and her spirit with Your limitless love.

Amen.

Deliverance from Temptation | 71

If you think you are standing firm,
be careful that you don't fall! No temptation
has overtaken you except what is common
to mankind. And God is faithful; He will
not let you be tempted beyond what you can
bear. But when you are tempted, He will also
provide a way out so that you can endure it.

1 Corinthians 10:12-13

Lord,

Keep my daughter from overconfidence
in her young faith, thinking she'll never fall.
Draw her close so she'll depend on Your
strength to stand firm. Give her wisdom to
recognize the enemy's schemes. Deliver her
from any temptation that will keep her
from living in obedience to You.

Amen.

72 | A Pure Heart & Mind

Flee the evil desires of youth
and pursue righteousness, faith,
love and peace, along with those who
call on the Lord out of a pure heart.

2 Timothy 2:22

Father,

Fill my daughter with longing for You. Let
her seek stronger faith, greater obedience
and deeper love as she grows. Guard her
heart from pride, lust and selfishness that
will drive her away from You. Surround her
with encouragement and help in following
You so she can find peace that only You
supply. Let her remain pure of heart and
mind as she discovers Your love
that never fails.

Amen.

73

Keeping Her Safe

The LORD will keep you from all harm –
He will watch over your life; the LORD
will watch over your coming and going
both now and forevermore.

Psalm 121:7-8

Lord God,

Thank You for Your constant watch
over my daughter. She is never out of Your
reach, never out of Your sight, and never
too far for You to bring her home. Continue
to protect her by Your love and power.
Surround her with angels and shield her
from the evil one. Guide her steps and
let her cling to You as her loving Father.
Keep her under Your wing forever.

Amen.

74

Having Hope

May the God of hope fill you with all joy
and peace as you trust in Him, so that
you may overflow with hope by the
power of the Holy Spirit.

Romans 15:13

Lord Jesus,

You are the One that can calm any storm in
my daughter's life. No matter the difficulty
or uncertainty, help my daughter to trust
in You. Replace her worries with peace and
her discouragement with hope. Fill her with
Your Spirit so her faith will rise above any
fear. Thank You for the joy that You give,
even in the darkest days.

Amen.

Living in Peace | 75

The entire law is fulfilled in keeping this one
command: "Love your neighbor as yourself."
If you bite and devour each other, watch out
or you will be destroyed by each other.

Galatians 5:14-15

Father,

My daughter can at times be consumed
by her own needs and desires, caring for
herself above anyone else. Give her joy in
loving others. Keep her from selfishness that
competes for attention and blessings. Grow
kindness and generosity in her heart so
she can live in peace with everyone.
Transform her mind and spirit
with gratitude and trust in You.

Amen.

76 | Teach Her Self-Control

Now you must also rid yourselves of all such things as these: anger, rage, malice, slander, and filthy language from your lips.

Colossians 3:8

Lord,

It's tempting for my daughter to lash out when she's angry. When she gives way to her temper, she hurts even the ones she loves. Teach my daughter self-control so she's not ruled by her emotions. Guard her lips from hateful, ugly words and keep her from destructive behavior. Replace her rage with forgiveness and peace. Transform her heart so she's known for her patience and love.

Amen.

77

When She Wanders

"What do you think? If a man owns
a hundred sheep, and one of them wanders
away, will he not leave the ninety-nine
on the hills and go to look for the
one that wandered off?"

Matthew 18:12

Father,

The distractions of this world could easily
cause my daughter's faith in You to falter.
She could be tempted to live for herself
instead of Jesus. The enemy's lies could
persuade her to doubt Your Word. I know
she is precious to You – pursue her heart
and draw her close to Yourself. Rescue
her from sin, strengthen her belief in Your
truth, and let her know Your love.

Amen.

78

Her Passions

Do not love the world or anything in the world. If anyone loves the world, love for the Father is not in them. For everything in the world – the lust of the flesh, the lust of the eyes, and the pride of life – comes not from the Father but from the world.

1 John 2:15-16

Lord God,

The world competes for my daughter's heart and mind. It tantalizes her with pleasure, possessions and pride that will only turn her away from You. Give her wisdom to see that the world's form of happiness is an illusion – true joy is only found in You. Fill her with Your love and a faith that can't be shaken. Be her greatest desire.

Amen.

Speaking Up for Others | 79

Speak up for those who cannot speak
for themselves, for the rights of all who
are destitute. Speak up and judge fairly;
defend the rights of the poor and needy.

Proverbs 31:8-9

Heavenly Father,

Thank You for Your justice that guards
the rights of the weak and the poor. Give
my daughter a courageous spirit to speak
up for those who can't defend themselves.
Use her to relieve suffering and restore
dignity. Fill her with mercy and compassion
for all people. Like Jesus, may she love the
unlovable and remember the forgotten.
Bless her for standing for the truth.

Amen.

80 | Courage in Times of Trouble

"The LORD Himself goes before you
and will be with you; He will never leave
you nor forsake you. Do not be afraid;
do not be discouraged."

Deuteronomy 31:8

Father,

My daughter is scared to face the changes
and challenges before her. Fear is suppres-
sing excitement and hope for the future.
Inspire her with confidence that You'll never
leave her side. Help her to trust that You're
in control and have wonderful plans in store
for her life. Give her courage to follow
wherever You lead, knowing she'll
never walk alone.

Amen.

81

Letting Go of Anger

"In your anger do not sin": Do not let the
sun go down while you are still angry,
and do not give the devil a foothold.

Ephesians 4:26-27

Lord,

My daughter is sometimes tempted to hold
on to anger and resentment toward others.
She can refuse to let go of the past and to
forgive. By Your Spirit, please replace the
bitterness with love. Keep the enemy from
hardening her heart. Help her to always lay
down the grudge she's carrying. Set her free
from anger today to live in peace tomorrow.

Amen.

82

Spiritual Growth

Like newborn babies, crave pure
spiritual milk, so that by it you may grow
up in your salvation, now that you have
tasted that the Lord is good.

1 Peter 2:2-3

Father,

My daughter's faith needs nourishment to
grow. Give her a hunger for Your Word, so
she can grow in Your truth. Let her taste and
see how good You are. May she seek Your
face in prayer and learn to recognize Your
voice. Surround her with other believers
to teach, pray and encourage my child to
follow You. Enable me to live in faithful
obedience as an example in her life.

Amen.

A Respectful Attitude | 83

Have confidence in your leaders
and submit to their authority, because
they keep watch over you as those who must
give an account. Do this so that their work
will be a joy, not a burden, for that would
be of no benefit to you.

Hebrews 13:17

Lord,

Thank You for placing authorities
over my daughter's life to teach, serve,
and protect her from harm. Help her
to appreciate the time and energy their
positions demand. Humble her heart to
submit to her leaders' rules and instruction,
trusting they're for her good. Make her
a blessing by her respectful attitude.
Reward her obedience with Your love.

Amen.

84 | Sexual Purity

Flee from sexual immorality.
All other sins a person commits are outside
the body, but whoever sins sexually,
sins against their own body.

1 Corinthians 6:18

Lord God,

In this world that distorts the beauty of
sexual intimacy, keep my daughter pure
in body and mind. Protect her innocence
and give her the strength to turn away from
any kind of immorality. Give her wisdom to
understand that her husband's love is worth
waiting for. Devote her heart to You so she
can live in pure obedience to Your Word.

Amen.

85

Encouragement & Strength

Praise be to the God and Father of our
Lord Jesus Christ, the Father of compassion
and the God of all comfort, who comforts
us in all our troubles, so that we can comfort
those in any trouble with the comfort
we ourselves receive from God.

2 Corinthians 1:3-4

Holy Lord,

My daughter is tired and troubled. Embrace
her with love – may she know You as her
comfort, help and strength. Use the difficul-
ties she suffers to create compassion for
others going through hard times. Let her
share the encouragement she receives from
You, becoming a blessing as she is blessed.
Thank You for Your love that never fails.

Amen.

86

Loving Others

"If you love those who love you, what reward will you get? Are not even the tax collectors doing that? And if you greet only your own people, what are you doing more than others? Do not even pagans do that?"

Matthew 5:46-47

Father,

Give my daughter a loving heart for everyone, even if they don't love her in return. Lift her eyes to see past her own circle of friends. Give her courage to reach out to others. Fill her with compassion for the unpopular, the unwelcome and the unlovely. Use my daughter's kindness and respect to shine the light of Jesus wherever she goes.

Amen.

A Teachable Heart | 87

The way of fools seems right to them,
but the wise listen to advice.

Proverbs 12:15

Lord,

My daughter has choices – to be wise
or foolish, humble or proud, yielding or
stubborn. Give her a teachable heart that
welcomes advice. Help her to understand
the limits of her experience and knowledge.
Protect her from having to learn the hard
way, by trying to figure out life on her own.
Build up our relationship so my influence
can help her along the way.

Amen.

88 | Finding True Happiness

I know what it is to be in need,
and I know what it is to have plenty.
I have learned the secret of being content in
any and every situation, whether well fed or
hungry, whether living in plenty or in want.

Philippians 4:12

Heavenly Father,

It's tempting for my daughter to depend
on "stuff" to feel happy and secure. She
becomes obsessed about what she'd like
to buy, and she pressures me to make every
wish come true. Teach her the secret of
being content. Set her free in knowing she
can find joy, no matter what she's gained
or lost. Give her gratitude for all the ways
You pour love into her life.

Amen.

89

Godly Role Models

Remember your leaders, who spoke the
word of God to you. Consider the outcome
of their way of life and imitate their faith.
Jesus Christ is the same yesterday and today
and forever. Do not be carried away by
all kinds of strange teachings.

Hebrews 13:7-9

Lord,

My daughter needs good judgment
in choosing her role models. Surround
my daughter with spiritual examples who
will show the way in following You. Give
her eyes to see their obedience, purity and
wisdom as they live for Jesus. Protect her
from anyone who would turn her away from
Your Word. Let my own faith and love for
You be worth imitating as I lead my child.

Amen.

90

Her Future Husband

Husbands, love your wives,
just as Christ loved the church
and gave Himself up for her.

Ephesians 5:25

Holy Lord,

In Your perfect plans for the future,
provide a loving husband for my daughter.
Let him be fully devoted to You and Your
Word. Prepare him even now to serve
and protect his family. Give him a heart
like Jesus so he can surrender his pride and
selfish desires. Fill him with Your love that
will overflow into his home. Bless him
as he cherishes my daughter.

Amen.

Focusing Her Thoughts on God | 91

Finally, brothers and sisters,
whatever is true, whatever is noble, whatever
is right, whatever is pure, whatever is lovely,
whatever is admirable – if anything is
excellent or praiseworthy –
think about such things.

Philippians 4:8

Father,

Transform my daughter's mind by Your
Spirit. Protect her from lies and confusion by
the knowledge of Your truth. Let her dream
of pleasing You with her goals and plans.
Give her a grace-filled perspective to see
the good in other people. Help her to
discern between what's pure and sinful,
noble and corrupt, beautiful and broken.
Captivate my daughter's thoughts
with Jesus.

Amen.

92 | Speaking Words of Blessing

Do not let any unwholesome talk come out of your mouths, but only what is helpful for building others up according to their needs, that it may benefit those who listen.

Ephesians 4:29

Father God,

Teach my daughter to understand the power of her words. Let her speak words of blessing instead of tearing others down. Guard her lips from profanity, gossip, lies and slander. Give her wisdom to know when to speak and when to stay silent. Help her to bring love, encouragement and truth to every conversation. Fill her mouth with truth and praise to Your name.

Amen.

93

Confessing Secret Sins

Then I acknowledged my sin to You
and did not cover up my iniquity. I said,
"I will confess my transgressions to the
LORD." And You forgave the guilt of my sin.

Psalm 32:5

Lord,

When my daughter sins, embarrassment,
stubbornness and shame often keep her
from confessing her sins to You. Encourage
her heart to trust in Your mercy. Let her
discover the freedom and peace that come
from bringing her guilt to You. Give her a
joyful heart as she receives Your forgiveness
and love. Thank You for Your mercy
and grace in her life.

Amen.

94

Overcoming Her Doubts

Yet he did not waver through
unbelief regarding the promise of God, but
was strengthened in his faith and gave glory
to God, being fully persuaded that God had
power to do what He had promised.

Romans 4:20-21

Father,

Help my daughter to believe Your promises –
that Jesus is alive and coming again, that
Your love never fails, and that Your Word is
forever true. The world will assault her faith
and the enemy will try to steal her hope.
Help her to stand firm so she can trust You
without wavering. Overcome her doubts
and help her to keep her eyes on You. Let
her see Your power, and praise You forever.

Amen.

Her Church Family | 95

Let us consider how we may spur one another
on toward love and good deeds, not giving
up meeting together, as some are in the habit
of doing, but encouraging one another – and
all the more as you see the Day approaching.

Hebrews 10:24-25

Lord Jesus,

In these dark days, my daughter
needs the encouragement of God's
people. Fill her with love for Your church.
Use other believers to set an example of
love and holiness for my child. Let her find
a place to belong in Your spiritual family,
so she never has to walk this life alone.
Make us faithful to each other until
You come and take us home.

Amen.

96 | Staying on the Path of Purity

How can a young person stay on the path
of purity? By living according to Your word.
I seek You with all my heart; do not let me
stray from Your commands.

Psalm 119:9-10

Father,

My daughter can receive mixed messages
about who she is and how she's supposed
to live. Clear up the confusion by giving
her a love for Your Word. Deepen her
understanding of the Scriptures. Let her
find direction, wisdom and truth as she
seeks You. Keep her feet on the path of
purity as she obeys You in every way.
Capture her heart and hold her close.

Amen.

97

Being an Example for Others

Don't let anyone look down on you because
you are young, but set an example for the
believers in speech, in conduct, in love,
in faith and in purity.

1 Timothy 4:12

Lord,

Thank You that my daughter can know You,
growing in faith and wisdom even as a child.
Let her speak words of truth and love like
Jesus. Give her an excellent reputation as
she obeys Your Word. Keep her faithful and
pure as she faces the challenges of growing
up. Use her life as an example to everyone
as she loves You more and more.

Amen.

98

Choosing the Right Friends

The righteous choose their friends carefully,
but the way of the wicked leads them astray.

Proverbs 12:26

Lord God,

Give my daughter wisdom to choose
the right friends, who will build her up and
bring her closer to You. Set her free from
the traps of popularity and pressure to
conform. Protect her from anyone who
would wound her spirit and discourage her
faith. Provide her with friends who love You
as their Savior. Thank You for being the
best Friend she'll ever know.

Amen.

Her Needs | 99

My God will meet all your needs according
to the riches of His glory in Christ Jesus.

Philippians 4:19

Father,

You know everything that my daughter
needs for health, knowledge and security.
Help her to trust You in every situation
because You care for her. Let her bring
every concern to You in prayer, and out
of Your riches give more than she could
hope for. Build her faith and hope in
Your amazing love as You provide. Thank
You for holding her life in Your hands.

Amen.

100 | Her Source of Rest

"Come to Me, all you who are weary
and burdened, and I will give you rest.
Take My yoke upon you and learn from Me,
for I am gentle and humble in heart, and
you will find rest for your souls. For My yoke
is easy and My burden is light."

Matthew 11:28-30

Heavenly Father,

My daughter is exhausted from
striving to become all she hopes to be.
She chases beauty, success and perfection.
Release her from the pressure. Let her
receive the love and mercy that You so freely
give. Help her to put her life in Your hands,
letting You lead the way. Be her source
of love and righteousness as
she puts her trust in You.

Amen.

101

Dependence on God

"Remain in Me, as I also remain in you.
No branch can bear fruit by itself; it must
remain in the vine. Neither can you bear
fruit unless you remain in Me. I am the vine;
you are the branches. If you remain in Me
and I in you, you will bear much fruit;
apart from Me you can do nothing."

John 15:4-5

Lord God,

Teach my daughter to depend on You for
everything. Let her lean on Your strength
to obey, and Your Word for the truth. Save
her from pride in her own goodness and
accomplishments. Draw her close and keep
her faithful. Keep her from forgetting You
and making her way alone. Let the fruit of
love and righteousness be borne in her
life as she remains in You.

Amen.